THE OFFICIAL itv SPORT
FORMULA ONE
ANNUAL 2008

Written by David Clayton
Designed by Simon Thorley

GRANADA

Ventures

ITV Sport is the exclusive broadcaster of FORMULA ONE in the UK.

The ITV Sport logo is licensed by Granada Ventures Ltd.

All rights reserved.

A Grange Publication

© 2007. Published by Grange Communications Ltd., Edinburgh, under licence from Granada Ventures Ltd. Printed in the EU.

Photographs © Action Images
ISBN 978-1-906211-02-8

£6.99

CONTENTS

AERODYNAMICS

This is the study of the airflow over and around a Formula 1 car. Designers spend a lot of time ensuring that the latest cars have as little wind resistance as possible.

APEX

The apex is the central point of the inside lane that drivers direct their cars at when turning corners.

APPEAL

F1 teams can make an appeal if they feel their driver has been harshly penalised by race officials.

BALLAST

Ballast is weights that are fixed in specific areas of the cars to achieve the best balance possible for safety

reasons. Each F1 car must also be at least equal to the minimum weight requirements.

BARGEBOARD

This is a part of the car body located between the front wheels to help ensure there is a smooth airflow around the side of the car.

BLISTERING

A tyre can blister when it becomes too hot. When this happens, parts of the tyre can break away and this can happen for various reasons, one of which is the wrong type of tyre for a particular circuit or the tyre pressure being too high.

BOTTOMING

This is caused by the chassis of the car hitting the track.

BRAKE BALANCE

There is a switch in the cockpit drivers can use to switch the brake power from the front to the rear, or vice versa.

CHASSIS

The chassis is the main section of the car – its spine – to which the engine and suspension are attached.

CHICANE

A chicane is a sequence of corners, close together in alternate directions that are often in place to slow cars down before sections of the track that could be dangerous, such as a high-speed corner.

CLEAN AIR

Usually experienced only by the car in front! The air behind the leader and the rest of the cars is turbulent and can affect the aerodynamics needed to achieve the smoothest drive.

COCKPIT

Where the driver sits and the hub of all the car's controls, located on the chassis.

COMPOUND

The ingredients of the car's tyres, vital to the safety of the driver and specially designed to achieve maximum speed, durability and grip in various weather conditions. A typical F1 car tyre will contain more than 10 different ingredients!

DOWNFORCE

This is the aerodynamic force that pushes down on the car as it travels at speed. Harnessed correctly, this can improve a car's handling, especially around corners.

DRAG

This is the aerodynamic resistance that hits the car as it moves along.

DRIVE-THROUGH-PENALTY

This is one of the two penalties that can be given to drivers during a race. If awarded, the offending driver must drive into the pit lane, continue through without stopping – but adhering to the lane's speed limit – then rejoin the race.

FLAT SPOT

The part of a tyre affected by a spin or extreme braking. This can ruin the car's handling and often causes the need for a tyre change.

FORMATION LAP

This is a lap involving all the participating cars starting at the grid and finishing at the grid with all cars in their correct starting position for the start of the race.

G-FORCE

A physical force experienced by drivers that can be felt while cornering, accelerating or braking.

GRAINING

Tiny bits of rubber that break away from the tyres that become stuck in the tread.

GRAVEL TRAP

A bed of gravel located on the outside of corners, designed for bringing cars that veer off the track to a safe stop.

INSTALLATION LAP

A necessary lap on arrival at a circuit to test functions such as the throttle, steering and brakes before returning to the pits – without crossing the finishing line.

JUMP START

Sensors detect if a driver moves away from his start position before five red lights are showing and if he does, a penalty is imposed.

LOLLIPOP

This is a sign held on a stick in front of a car during a pit stop. It indicates the driver must apply the brakes, engage first gear before the car is lowered off its jacks.

DRIVERPROFILES

FERNANDO ALONSO

TEAM: MCLAREN
BORN: 29/7/81
NATIONALITY: SPANISH
BIRTHPLACE: OVIEDO, SPAIN
WORLD CHAMPIONSHIPS: 2
HIGHEST FINISH: 1
RACE WINS: 18

FELIPE MASSA

TEAM: FERRARI
BORN: 25/4/81
NATIONALITY: BRAZILIAN
BIRTHPLACE: SAO PAULO, BRAZIL
WORLD CHAMPIONSHIPS: 0
HIGHEST FINISH: 1
RACE WINS: 4

KIMI RÄIKKÖNEN

TEAM: FERRARI
BORN: 17/10/79
NATIONALITY: FINNISH
BIRTHPLACE: ESPOO, FINLAND
WORLD CHAMPIONSHIPS: 0
HIGHEST FINISH: 1
RACE WINS: 12

VITANTONIO LIUZZI

TEAM: TORRO ROSSO
BORN: 8/6/81
NATIONALITY: ITALIAN
BIRTHPLACE: LOCOROTONDO
WORLD CHAMPIONSHIPS: 0
HIGHEST FINISH: 8
RACE WINS: 0

DETAILS CORRECT TO 14/8/07

Australian Grand Prix

Albert Park

Address: Australian Grand Prix
Corporation, 220 Albert Road,
Melbourne, Victoria 3125, Australia
First Race: 1996
Circuit Length: 5.303 Km
Laps: 58

1

Bahrain Grand Prix

Bahrain International Racing Circuit

Address: Sakhir Circuit, P.O. Box 26381, Manama, Kingdom of Bahrain
First Race: 2004
Circuit Length: 5.417 Km
Laps: 57

SPOT THE DIFFERENCE ?

Picture A is different from Picture B – can you find and circle the 6 changes we've made in Picture B?

A

B

LEWIS
HAMILTON

TEAM:
MCLAREN

BORN:
7/1/85

NATIONALITY:
BRITISH

BIRTHPLACE:
STEVENAGE, ENGLAND

WORLD CHAMPIONSHIPS:
0

HIGHEST FINISH:
1

RACE WINS:
3

HEIGHT:
1.74M

WEIGHT:
68KG

HOBBIES:
**PLAYING THE GUITAR,
MUSIC, TRAINING**

OFFICIAL WEBSITE:
WWW.LEWISHAMILTON.COM

GRAND PRIX DEBUT:
**2007 AUSTRALIAN
GRAND PRIX**

DETAILS CORRECT TO 14/8/07

LEWIS CARL HAMILTON was born on January 7, 1985 in Stevenage and was named after the legendary USA sprinter Carl Lewis – how ironic that Lewis himself would become one of the fastest men on the planet in future years! His father, Anthony, bought him a go-kart aged six and the youngster showed great enthusiasm and aptitude even at such a tender age. His race career started at the age of eight, and, like many other F1 drivers, he started by racing karts and at the age of nine, he approached McLaren F1 team boss Ron Dennis at an awards ceremony and told him he would drive for McLaren one day! Self-confidence was never something he lacked! His dad took on up to three jobs at one stage to help finance his son's fledgling career and despite the workload, he managed to attend all of Lewis' races . ▶

Lewis was a multi-talented sports enthusiast and by the age of 12 he'd won a black belt at Karate, a form of self-defence he'd originally started to protect himself from local bullies who were jealous of his racing talents. He also played football for the school team alongside future Aston Villa striker Ashley Young – there seemed no end to his talents! Within four years, Lewis had been signed on to the McLaren driver development support programme. Inspired by the professional tuition and advice he'd craved, he became the European karting champion

I think Lewis is going to rewrite the book. We'll see a new generation of what I call properly prepared, professional racing drivers. I believe Lewis will create the benchmark for a whole generation of drivers **Sir Jackie Stewart**

in 2000 just a year later, aged 15. The rising star then progressed to cars just over a year later and his success continued with maximum points and he made the successful transition to racing cars the following year. He won titles in Formula Renault, Formula

3 and GP2 and was appointed as a Formula 1 driver for McLaren in 2007, just as he'd said he would some 13 years earlier and in doing so, he became the youngest ever driver to secure an F1 contract. His first ever F1 race was in the 2007 Australian Grand Prix, where

he started fourth on the grid and finished third in the race becoming only the fourteenth rookie driver to finish on the podium on his debut. He finished second in his second race in Malaysia and held pole position for the first time, eventually finishing second behind Brazil's Felipe Massa – it was a repeat one-two in the Spanish Grand Prix and the points gained enabled Lewis to move to the top of the world drivers' championship – the youngest ever driver to do so! The inevitable had to happen and in the Canadian Grand Prix,

Lewis led virtually from start to finish to claim his first F1 victory and a week later he repeated the success, winning the US Grand Prix in Indianapolis but his dream of winning on home soil didn't come true on his debut at Silverstone, where, despite leading for the first part of the race, he finished third in front of more than 80,000 adoring fans. It will come, Lewis, don't worry. With youth on his side, a fantastic personality and plenty of talent, Lewis Hamilton could yet become the greatest F1 driver Britain has ever seen.
Triple world champion Sir Jackie

Stewart said:"I think Lewis is going to rewrite the book. We'll see a new generation of what I call properly prepared, professional racing drivers. I believe Lewis will create the benchmark for a whole generation of drivers. Niki Lauda and James Hunt changed the culture of racing drivers, but they weren't role models. Lewis Hamilton can become a role model."
F1 supremo Bernie Ecclestone also believes Lewis can go on to great things in future years. He said: "Lewis had got a lot of talent. The guy's a winner."

DETAILS CORRECT TO 14/8/07

PITSTOP

Think the F1 drivers are under pressure? What about the crews of technicians and mechanics who need to perform their high pressure duties in a matter of seconds? Get it wrong and the race is

1.5 Seconds

A fuelling hose is inserted into the tank nozzle. A red light inside the refueller's helmet visor indicates an optimum fuel flow of 12 litres per second

2.5 Seconds

The wheels are expertly removed

1.0 Seconds

A hydraulic jack lifts the front of the car while a manual jack lifts the rear

0.2 Seconds

A high-powered airgun is applied to the centre wheel nuts

0.0 Seconds

The car stops and the clock begins to tick

as good as over, but get it right every time and you might just be the deciding factor in the race. Below are the tasks a typical pit-stop crew will undertake and all the while, the clock is tick, tick, ticking...

3.5 Seconds

The new wheels are mounted and the central wheel nuts are refitted and tightened

3.8 Seconds

The car is lowered off the jacks

4.3 Seconds

The lollipop man signals the driver to engage 1st gear and apply brakes

7.0 Seconds

A green light in the refueller's helmet visor indicates required level reached and hose is disconnected

7.3 Seconds

Lollipop man signals driver to go and it's all over – in the blink of an eye the car is back to optimum operating levels and rejoins the race – job done!

F1 WORLD CIRCUITS

Belgian Grand Prix

Spa Francorchamps Circuit

③

Address: Circuit de Spa Francorchamps, Route du Circuit 55, 4970 Francorchamps, Belgium
First Race: 1983 (Revised Shorter Version)
Circuit Length: 6.968 Km
Laps: 44

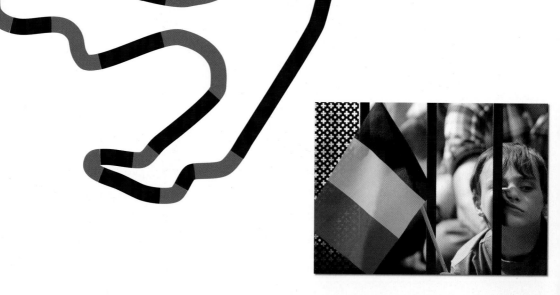

Brazilian Grand Prix

Autodromo Jose Carlos Pace

Address: Avenida Senador Teotonio
Vilela 261, 010000-000 Interlagos,
Sao Paulo, Brazil
First Race: 1973
Circuit Length: 4.309 Km
Laps: 71

4

THE BIG F1 QUIZ

1. **WHICH F1 GRAND PRIX HAS THE FEWEST LAPS?**

2. **WHAT IS THE NAME OF THE CANADIAN F1 CIRCUIT?**

3. **TRUE OF FALSE: F1 CHIEF BERNIE ECCLESTONE WAS BORN IN IRELAND**

4. **HOW MANY LAPS DOES IT TAKE TO COMPLETE THE SILVERSTONE F1 GRAND PRIX?**

5. **WHERE WOULD YOU FIND PADDLES ON A F1 CAR?**

6. **WHAT HAPPENS IF A DRIVER PERFORMS A JUMP START?**

7. **WHO WON THE 2007 BRITISH GRAND PRIX?**

8. **WHERE DID LEWIS HAMILTON WIN HIS FIRST F1 GRAND PRIX?**

9. **WHICH BRITISH DRIVER REPRESENTS RED BULL?**

10. **WHICH TYRE COMPANY SUPPLIES ALL FORMULA 1 CARS?**

11. **WHAT COLOUR IS THE SAFETY CAR?**

Answers on pg 58 & 59

12. IN 2007, HOW MANY F1 TEAMS WERE THERE?

13. WHAT ARE THE INITIALS OF F1'S GOVERNING BODY?

14. IN WHICH COUNTY IS SILVERSTONE LOCATED? OXFORDSHIRE OR NORTHAMPTONSHIRE?

15. MONACO HAS THE MOST AMOUNT OF LAPS OF ANY F1 WORLD CIRCUIT. TRUE OR FALSE?

16. WHO WAS THE F1 WORLD CHAMPION IN 2005 AND 2006?

17. WHERE WAS JENSON BUTTON BORN? SOMERSET OR DORSET?

18. HOW MANY SECONDS DOES A 'STOP-GO' PENALTY LAST?

19. WHAT IS USED TO KEEP TYRES AT THE OPTIMUM RACE TEMPERATURE PRIOR TO FITTING?

20. WHERE IS THE MANUAL JACK USED DURING A PIT-STOP? FRONT OR BACK OF THE CAR?

DRIVERPROFILES

TAKUMA SATO

TEAM: SUPER AGURI
BORN: 28/1/77
NATIONALITY: JAPANESE
BIRTHPLACE: TOKYO, JAPAN
WORLD CHAMPIONSHIPS: 0
HIGHEST FINISH: 3
RACE WINS: 0

ALEXANDER WURZ

TEAM: WILLIAMS
BORN: 15/2/74
NATIONALITY: AUSTRIAN
BIRTHPLACE: WAIDHOFEN THAYA, AUSTRIA
WORLD CHAMPIONSHIPS: 0
HIGHEST FINISH: 3
RACE WINS: 0

NICO ROSBERG

TEAM: WILLIAMS
BORN: 27/6/85
NATIONALITY: GERMAN
BIRTHPLACE: WIESBADEN
WORLD CHAMPIONSHIPS: 0
HIGHEST FINISH: 6
RACE WINS: 0

GIANCARLO FISICHELLA

TEAM: RENAULT
BORN: 14/1/73
NATIONALITY: ITALIAN
BIRTHPLACE: ROME, ITALY
WORLD CHAMPIONSHIPS: 0
HIGHEST FINISH: 1
RACE WINS: 3

DETAILS CORRECT TO 14/8/07

JENSON BUTTON

TEAM:
HONDA

BORN:
19/1/80

NATIONALITY:
BRITISH

BIRTHPLACE:
FROME, SOMERSET

WORLD CHAMPIONSHIPS:
0

HIGHEST FINISH:
1

RACE WINS:
1

JENSON BUTTON was born and raised in Frome, Somerset, the son of Rallycross ace John Button. Jenson began karting aged eight, after his father bought him his first go-kart and his talent quickly shone through as he made an incredible start to his young career, becoming British Cadet Kart Champion after wining all 34 races. Further successes followed, including three triumphs in the British Open Kart Championship and in 1997 he became the youngest driver ever to win the European Super A Championship, winning the Ayrton Senna Memorial Cup as well.

Aged 18, he contested the British Formula Ford Championship with Haywood Racing and won the title with nine race wins. He also triumphed in the Formula Ford Festival at Brands Hatch, ahead of future Indianapolis 500 winner Dan Wheldon. Such successes didn't go unnoticed and in 1998 he was awarded the McLaren Autosport Young Driver Award and part of his prize included a test in a McLaren

Formula 1 car, which he received at the end of the following year. Jenson entered Formula Three in 1999 with the Promatecme team. He won three times - at Thruxton, Pembrey and Silverstone - and finished the season as top rookie driver. He joined Williams after winning a race-off for a vacant driver's seat and went on to finish eighth in the 2000 Drivers' Championship, with his best finish a fourth-placed effort during an impressive first season. Jenson has driven for Benetton (later to become Renault F1) but finished in a disappointing 17th in his first year with them, but in 2002 he achieved his best-ever finish of seventh in the Drivers' Championship.

He was replaced in 2003 at Renault by another driver. He joined the BAR team (later to become Honda Racing F1), alongside former world champion Jacques Villeneuve and Jenson's best result of the season was fourth place in Austria and he finished ninth in the Drivers' Championship that year with 17 points.

In 2004, Button and BAR-Honda made significant progress and BAR finished the season second in the Constructors' Championship. Button scored his first ever podium finish with a third place in the Malaysian Grand Prix, and added several more throughout the season.

His first pole position came in April at the 2004 San Marino Grand

Prix, in which he finished second. He ended the season third overall in the Drivers' Championship – a fantastic achievement - and in 2006, he celebrated his first ever F1 victory after success in the Hungarian Grand Prix and he finished the season in sixth spot overall with 56 points.

In 2007, Jenson again competed with the Honda Racing F1 team alongside Rubens Barrichello, but a rib injury held back his progress after he was unable to participate in crucial winter testing prior to the new F1 season. Clearly, Jenson has the talent, but whether he will ever contest to be world champion or not may depend on the car he drives in future years.

British Grand Prix

Silverstone Circuit

Address: Silverstone International Circuit, Northamptonshire, NN12 8TN, United Kingdom
First Race: 1950
Circuit Length: 5.141 Km
Laps: 60

⑤

Canadian Grand Prix

Circuit Gilles Villeneuve

Address: Bassin Olympique, Ile de
Notre-Dame, Montreal, Quebec
H2Y 3G7, Canada
First Race: 1978
Circuit Length: 4.361 Km
Laps: 70

F1 **CROSSWORD**PUZZLE

You'll need all your knowledge on Formula One to solve the crossword puzzle below. Answer the questions, fill in the blanks and see if you can last the course

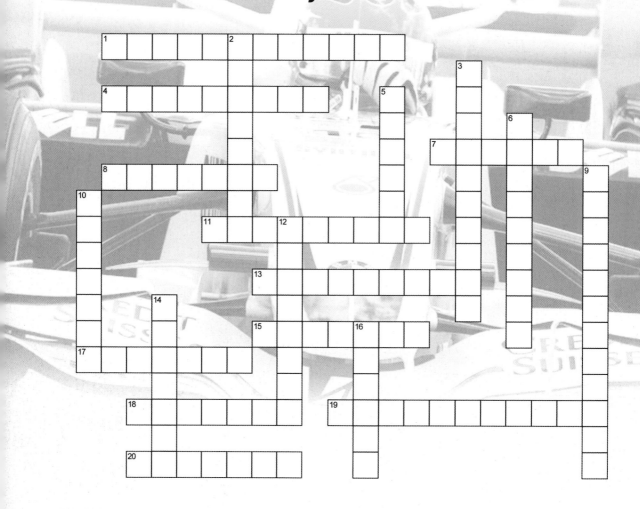

ACROSS

1 Where every driver wants to start the race (4,8)
4 Cars are weighed in this area (4,5)
7 Location of Malaysian circuit (6)
8 Course official (7)
11 Reward for finishing first (3,6)
13 Town where Lewis Hamilton was born (9)
15 Where the driver sits (7)
17 A driver can be imposed one of these if he commits an offence during the race (7)
18 Country Kimi Raikkonen was born in (7)
19 British F1 circuit (11)
20 A tight sequence of corners (7)

DOWN

2 A move to get ahead of the driver in front (8)
3 What the man in the car at the front is called prior to finish (4,6)
5 You're not allowed to race unless you wear this on your head (6)
6 You'll see this vehicle driving on the track when there is a problem (6,3)
9 Top German driver 2007 (4,8)
10 Where the drivers head for when they have problems (3,4)
12 This is held up so a driver knows his position (3,5)
14 Fernando Alonso's nationality (7)
16 Place all drivers want to stand at the end of the race! (6)

Answers on pg 58 & 59

DRIVERPROFILES

RUBENS BARRICHELLO

TEAM: HONDA
BORN: 23/5/72
NATIONALITY: BRAZILIAN
BIRTHPLACE: SAO PAULO, BRAZIL
WORLD CHAMPIONSHIPS: 0
HIGHEST FINISH: 1
RACE WINS: 9

RALF SCHUMACHER

TEAM: TOYOTA
BORN: 30/6/75
NATIONALITY: GERMAN
BIRTHPLACE: HÜRTH-HERMÜLHEIM, GERMANY
WORLD CHAMPIONSHIPS: 0
HIGHEST FINISH: 1
RACE WINS: 6

SCOTT SPEED

TEAM: TORRO ROSSO
BORN: 24/1/83
NATIONALITY: AMERICAN
BIRTHPLACE: MANTECA, USA
WORLD CHAMPIONSHIPS: 0
HIGHEST FINISH: 9
RACE WINS: 0

MARK WEBBER

TEAM: RED BULL
BORN: 27/8/76
NATIONALITY: AUSTRALIAN
BIRTHPLACE: QUEANBEYAN, AUSTRALIA
WORLD CHAMPIONSHIPS: 0
HIGHEST FINISH: 3
RACE WINS: 0

DETAILS CORRECT TO 9/7/07

F1 WORLD CIRCUITS

Chinese Grand Prix

Shanghai Circuit

Address: Shanghai International
Racing Circuit, 1558 Dingxi Road,
Shanghai, China
First Race: 2004
Circuit Length: 5.451 Km
Laps: 58

7

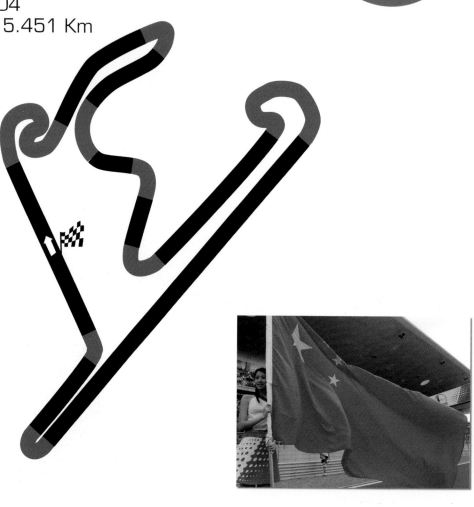

French Grand Prix

Circuit de Magny Cours

Address: Circuit de Nevers Magny
Cours, Technopole, F - 58470
Magny Cours, France
First Race: 1991
Circuit Length: 4.408 Km
Laps: 50

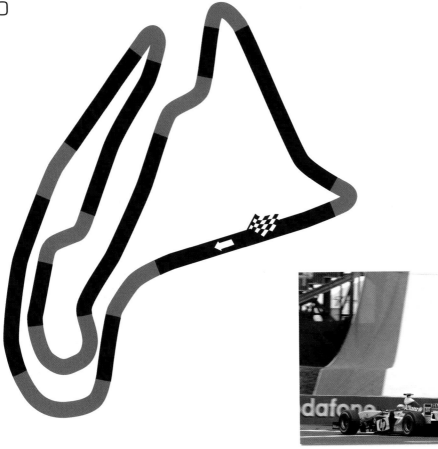

WORDSEARCH

Can you circle 10 words associated with F1 in the grid below? The words can be found upwards, downwards, backwards, forwards, sideways or diagonal – good luck!

```
N O I S N E P S U S Z R
X G S V T V Z K N C T L
X Q G E N W R M G I L T
E P R H R E K H E M M I
N N L X V Y E H A A G U
G N G I D L T T R N Y C
F M R I M J I Z B Y M R
D D N E N P D T O D W I
G Y T Z K E H V X O T C
T B R C H E Q U E R E D
R T O K F K W V T E N Q
Y C F F N R X H F A R N
```

Answers on pg 58 & 59

DAVID
COULTHARD

TEAM:
RED BULL

BORN:
27/3/71

NATIONALITY:
BRITISH

BIRTHPLACE:
TWYNHOLM, SCOTLAND

WORLD CHAMPIONSHIPS:
0

HIGHEST FINISH:
1

RACE WINS:
13

DETAILS CORRECT TO 14/8/07

LIKE SO MANY F1 drivers, David Coulthard began racing by driving go-karts as a youngster and won the Scottish championship several times and then the British championship. In 1989 he won a Formula Ford 1600 championship, and in 1991 he finished second in the British Formula 3 series. As his career progressed apace, he added two Formula 3 titles to his list of successes, winning the Macau Grand Prix and the Marlboro Masters. He raced in Formula 3000 in 1992 and 1993, finishing ninth the first year and third in the second year.

David had an unfortunate path into F1 when he was hired by Williams as a replacement for Ayrton Senna who was tragically killed in an accident at the San Marino Grand Prix on May 1, 1994. He managed one podium finish in his first year and finished eight in the Drivers' Championship with 14 points and since his first season has amassed more points than any other British driver in history over his career to date. Of the 13 races he's won, the most notable ones were undoubtedly the British Grand Prix, the Belgian Grand Prix at Spa-Francorchamps, the Italian Grand Prix at Monza, the French Grand Prix and above all, the Monaco Grand Prix, which he won in both 2000 and in 2002.

A steady driver, consistency has always been his strongest asset and David has picked up points for all the teams he has driven for over the years. He narrowly escaped death in 2000 when a private jet he and his fiancée were travelling on crashed in France killing the pilot and co-pilot. Both he and his fiancée escaped uninjured, though David made a valiant effort to save the lives of the pilots, there was little he could do with a fierce fire to contend with. Showing incredible mental strength, he finished second in the Spanish Grand Prix days later and then won in Monaco a month after that.

David now drives for Red Bull and is one of the most respected F1 drivers in the world.

F1 WORLD CIRCUITS

German Grand Prix

Nürburgring Circuit

Address: Nürburgring Circuit GmbH,
D53520 Nurburg, Germany
First Race: 1984
Circuit Length: 5.148 Km
Laps: 60

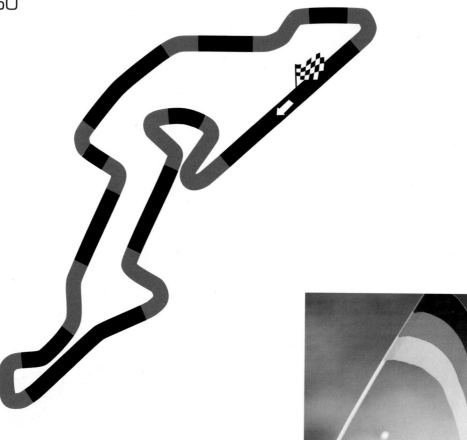

Hungarian Grand Prix

Hungaroring Circuit

Address: Hungaroring Circuit, Pf10,
H-2146 Mogyorod, Budapest,
Hungary
First Race: 1986
Circuit Length: 4.384 Km
Laps: 70

WHICH CIRCUIT?

Below are four images of Formula 1 circuits – use your detective work to figure out where they are in the world – remember, the clues are in the pictures...

1

3

GULF AIR طيران الخليج

Answers on pg 58 & 59

WHO AM I?

Can you guess who these four top F1 drivers are? We've disguised their identity so it won't be easy – can you solve the mystery?

Answers on pg 58 & 59

PIT-STOP CHALLENGE

Your car is low on fuel – can you work your way through the maze to find the pit-stop? One wrong turn and you could be out of the race!

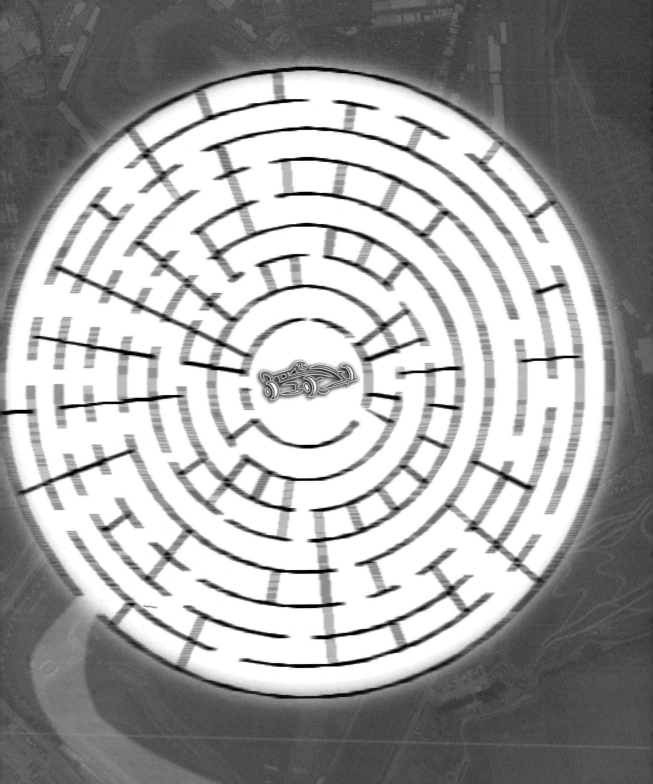

F1 WORLD CIRCUITS

Italian Grand Prix

Monza Circuit

Address: Monza Racing Circuit,
Parco di Monza, I-20052 Monza,
Italy
First Race: 1950
Circuit Length: 5.793 Km
Laps: 58

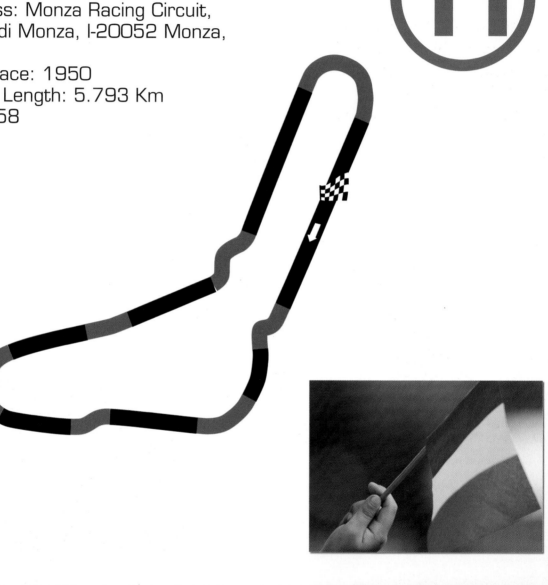

Japanese Grand Prix

Fuji International Speedway

Address: Fuji International
Speedway, Oyama Cho, Sunto Gun,
Shizuoka, 410-1308, Japan
First Race: 1976
Circuit Length: 4.549 Km
Laps: 67

SPOT THE DIFFERENCE ?

Picture A is different from Picture B – can you find and circle the 6 changes we've made in Picture B?

Answers on pg 58 & 59

DRIVERPROFILES

JARNO TRULLI
TEAM: TOYOTA
BORN: 13/7/74
NATIONALITY: ITALIAN
BIRTHPLACE: PESCARA
WORLD CHAMPIONSHIPS: 0
HIGHEST FINISH: 1
RACE WINS: 1

ROBERT KUBICA
TEAM: BMW SAUBER
BORN: 7/12/84
NATIONALITY: POLISH
BIRTHPLACE: KRAKOW, POLAND
WORLD CHAMPIONSHIPS: 0
HIGHEST FINISH: 3
RACE WINS: 0

Malaysian Grand Prix

Sepang International Circuit

Address: Circuit Management Centre, Jalan Pekeliling, Kuala Lumpur, 64100 KLIA, Selangor, Malaysia
First Race: 1999
Circuit Length: 5.543 Km
Laps: 56

Monaco Grand Prix

Circuit de Monaco

Address: Automobile Club de
Monaco, 23 Boulevard Albert 1er,
Monaco Cedex, MC 98012, Monte
Carlo
First Race: 1950
Circuit Length: 3.37 Km
Laps: 78

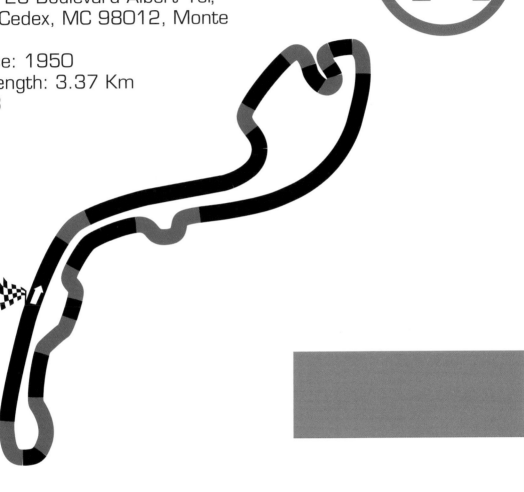

DRIVER PROFILES

CHRISTIJAN ALBERS
TEAM: SPYKER
BORN: 16/4/79
NATIONALITY: DUTCH
BIRTHPLACE: EINDHOVEN,
HOLLAND
WORLD CHAMPIONSHIPS: 0
HIGHEST FINISH: 5
RACE WINS: 0

HEIKKI KOVALAINEN
TEAM: RENAULT
BORN: 19/10/81
NATIONALITY: FINNISH
BIRTHPLACE: SUOMUSSALMI,
FINLAND
WORLD CHAMPIONSHIPS: 0
HIGHEST FINISH: 4
RACE WINS: 0

NICK HEIDFELD
TEAM: BMW SAUBER
BORN: 10/5/77
NATIONALITY: GERMAN
BIRTHPLACE: MONCHENGLADBACH,
GERMANY
WORLD CHAMPIONSHIPS: 0
HIGHEST FINISH: 2
RACE WINS: 0

ANTHONY DAVIDSON
TEAM: SUPER AGURI
BORN: 18/4/79
NATIONALITY: BRITISH
BIRTHPLACE: HEMEL HEMPSTEAD,
ENGLAND
WORLD CHAMPIONSHIPS: 0
HIGHEST FINISH: 11
RACE WINS: 0

DETAILS CORRECT TO 9/7/07

MARSHAL

F1's version of a referee. The marshal's job is to ensure the race runs smoothly and safely and he is also involved in spectator safety, acting as a fire warden when needed, helping to rescue stranded drivers or cars from the track as well as waving flags to signal the track condition to drivers – a busy man!

OVERSTEER

Often a result of turning a corner too quickly, it can be corrected by opposite lock steering by turning the front wheels into a skid.

PADDLES

These are levers located on either side of the rear of the steering wheel enabling the driver to change gear up and down – a sort of F1 gear-stick.

PARC FERME

This is a secure, fenced off area where cars are driven after they've qualified for the race. No team members are allowed to touch the cars, except under strict supervision of race stewards.

PIT BOARD

This is a board held out on a pit wall, informing a driver of his position in the race as well as how many laps remain.

PIT WALL

This is where the team owner, managers and engineers watch the race, often under some kind of cover to keep rain or bright sunshine off their monitors.

PITS

This is an area separated from the start/finish line by a straight wall. Cars enter the pits for general maintenance such as refuelling or tyre changes.

PLANK

A hard wooden strip fitted underneath all the F1 cars to indicate whether or not the car is being driven too low to the track surface – if the wood shows excessive damage, the problem needs to be rectified.

POLE POSITION

The aim of every driver and the first position on the starting grid awarded to the driver with the fastest lap recorded during qualification.

QUALIFYING

A knock-out session held on a Saturday where the drivers compete for the best times to decide where they will start on the grid.

RETIREMENT

A driver is forced to retire during a race if he suffers an irreversible mechanical failure or is involved in an accident.

SAFETY CAR

This is a course vehicle that is called from the pits and drives in front of the leading car in the event of an incident that means the cars need to be slowed down to a safe speed.

SIDEPOD

Part of the car that runs alongside the driver and runs to the rear wing, housing radiators.

SLIPSTREAMING

This is a tactic used by a driver whereby he catches the car in front, tucks in behind his rear wing therefore reducing the drag over the trailing car's body and opening the possibility of jettisoning past before the next corner.

SPLASH AND DASH

This is a pit stop taken by a car approaching the final few laps of the race whereby the driver requires just a few litres of fuel to complete the course.

STOP-GO PENALTY

A penalty in which a driver must return to his pit and stop for 10 seconds with no refuelling or tyre changes.

TELEMETRY

This is a system that beams information relating to the car's engine and chassis to computers in the pit-garage and enables engineers to monitor the car's performance.

TORQUE

The turning or twisting force of an engine generally used to measure an engine's flexibility. A powerful engine with little torque may actually be slower than a lesser engine with more torque on certain circuits – achieving the correct balance between the two is essential for a car to achieve continually good results.

TRACTION

This is the degree that a car is able to transfer power onto the track surface for forward momentum.

TYRE WARMER

This is, in effect, an electric blanket to keep tyres close to their optimum operating temperature prior to being fitted.

UNDERSTEER

This occurs when the front end of the car resists turning into a corner and slides wide as the driver attempts to turn towards the apex.

Spanish Grand Prix

Circuit de Catalunya

Address: Mas 'La Moreneta',
Apartado de Correos 27, E08160
Montmelo, Spain
First Race: 1991
Circuit Length: 4.627 Km
Laps: 66

Turkish Grand Prix

Istanbul Park Circuit

Address: Karaaliler Place, Tepeoren
Road, Akfirat County, Tuzla, Istanbul,
Turkey
First Race: 2005
Circuit Length: 5.34 Km
Laps: 58

QUIZ
ANSWERS

BIG QUIZ ANSWERS (P22):

01. BELGIUM
02. CIRCUIT GILLES VILLENEUVE
03. FALSE – HE WAS BORN IN SUFFOLK, ENGLAND
04. 60 LAPS
05. ON THE STEERING WHEEL
06. HE RECEIVES A PENALTY
07. KIMI RAIKKONEN
08. CANADA
09. DAVID COULTHARD
10. BRIDGESTONE
11. SILVER
12. 11 TEAMS
13. FIA
14. NORTHAMPTONSHIRE
15. TRUE – 78
16. FERNANDO ALONSO
17. SOMERSET
18. 10 SECONDS
19. TYRE WARMERS
20. BACK

WHICH CIRCUIT ANSWERS (P42)

1. SEPANG
2. BAHRAIN
3. FRANCE
4. AUSTRALIA

SPOT THE DIFFERENCE ANSWERS (P13)

01. ABBEY LOGO
02. SHELL LOGO
03. RED STRIP ON HELMET
04. ROOM OVERHANG SUPPORT
05. BRIDGESTONE LOGO
06. ROOF POLE

SPOT THE DIFFERENCE ANSWERS (P48)

01. BOSS LOGO
02. VODAFONE LOGO (LARGE)
03. PHOTOGRAPHERS HAND
04. NESCAFE LOGO ON DRINK
05. CLEAR STRAW
06. VODAFONE LOGO (SMALL)

Wordsearch Solution

```
N O I S N E P S U S Z R
X G S V T V Z K N C T L
X Q G E N W R M G I L T
E P R H R E K H E M I U
N N L X V Y E H A A G G
G N G I D L T T R N Y C
F M R I M J I Z B Y M R
D D N E N P D T O D W I
G Y T Z K E H V X O T C
T B R C H E Q U E R E D
R T O K F K W V T E N Q
Y C F F N R X H F A R N
```

▲
WORDSEARCH SOLUTION (P36)

Crossword Solution

```
P O L E P O S I T I O N
        V               R
  P A R C F E R M E   H   A
        R           E   C   S
        T           L   E   E P A N G
  M A R S H A L     M   A         N
  P       T E N P O I N T S       I
  I             B       D         C
  T         S T E V E N A G E     K
  S     S       B       R         H
  O     P   C O C K P I T         E
  P E N A L T Y     O             I
        N       P   D             D
    F I N L A N D   I   S I L V E R S T O N E
        S           U             L
    C H I C A N E   M             D
```

▲
CROSSWORD SOLUTION (P30)

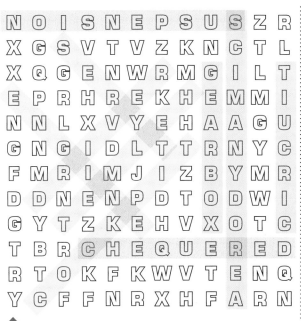

NICK
HEIDFELD

IMI
RAIKKONEN

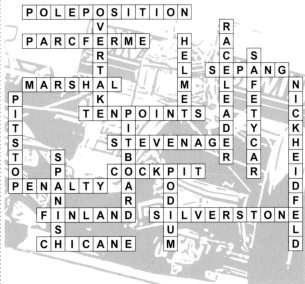

JENSON
BUTTON

WHO AM I? (P 43)

FERNANDO
ALONSO

PIT
STOP

KIMI
RAIKKONEN

FERNANDO
ALONSO

*MAZE SOLUTION
(P45)*

NICK
HEIDFELD

JENSON
BUTTON

United States Grand Prix

Indianapolis Motor Speedway

(17)

Address: Indianapolis Motor Speedway, 4790 West 16th Street, Indianapolis, IN 46222, USA
First Race: 2000
Circuit Length: 4.192 Km
Laps: 73